PRIMARY SOURCES IN AMERICAN HISTORY™

THE CONTINENTAL CONGRESS

A PRIMARY SOURCE HISTORY OF THE FORMATION OF AMERICA'S NEW GOVERNMENT

BETTY BURNETT, PH.D.

rosen central
Primary Source™

The Rosen Publishing Group, Inc., New York

Published in 2004 by The Rosen Publishing Group, Inc.
29 East 21st Street, New York, NY 10010

Library of Congress Cataloging-in-Publication Data

Burnett, Betty, 1940–
The Continental Congress: a primary source history of the formation of America's new government/by Betty Burnett.— 1st ed.
        p. cm.—(Primary sources in American history)
Summary: Uses primary source documents, narrative, and illustrations to recount the history of the colonies' break from Great Britain and the creation of a new government of the United States. Includes bibliographical references and index.
ISBN 0-8239-4510-3 (library binding)
1. United States. Continental Congress—Juvenile literature. 2. United States—Politics and government—1775-1783—Juvenile literature. 3. United States—Politics and government—1783-1789—Juvenile literature. [1. United States. Continental Congress—Sources. 2. United States—Politics and government—1775-1783—Sources. 3. United States—Politics and government—1783-1789-Sources.]
I. Title. II. Series.
E303.B89 2004
973.3'12—dc22

                                                                    2003013081

Manufactured in the United States of America

On the front cover: *Drafting the Declaration of Independence*, a 1776 painting by J. L. G. Ferris.

On the back cover: First row *(left to right)*: committee drafting the Declaration of Independence for action by the Continental Congress; Edward Braddock and troops ambushed by Indians at Fort Duquesne. Second row *(left to right)*: the *Mayflower* in Plymouth Harbor; the Oregon Trail at Barlow Cutoff. Third row *(left to right)*: slaves waiting at a slave market; the USS *Chesapeake* under fire from the HMS *Shannon*.

CONTENTS

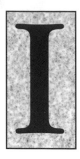NTRODUCTION

In 1775, about 2.5 million people lived in England's thirteen American colonies. The majority of residents were British subjects from Scotland, Ireland, Wales, and England. Scattered throughout the colonies were settlements of French, German, and Dutch people, as well as African slaves and Native Americans.

THE THIRTEEN COLONIES

The colonies were grouped into three sections. New England was made up of New Hampshire (including the territory of Vermont), Massachusetts, Connecticut, and Rhode Island. Boston was the largest city in New England and a major port. New Englanders were mostly farmers, merchants, and craftspeople. Their ties to church and community were strong, and they encouraged citizen participation in local government.

The middle colonies included New York, New Jersey, Pennsylvania, Delaware, and Maryland. With 28,000 inhabitants, Philadelphia was the largest city in the middle colonies and in America. Founded by Quakers, it was known for its tolerance of diversity. Twelve different religious denominations worshiped freely in this city of broad streets and neat brick homes. New York City, founded by the Dutch, was not as

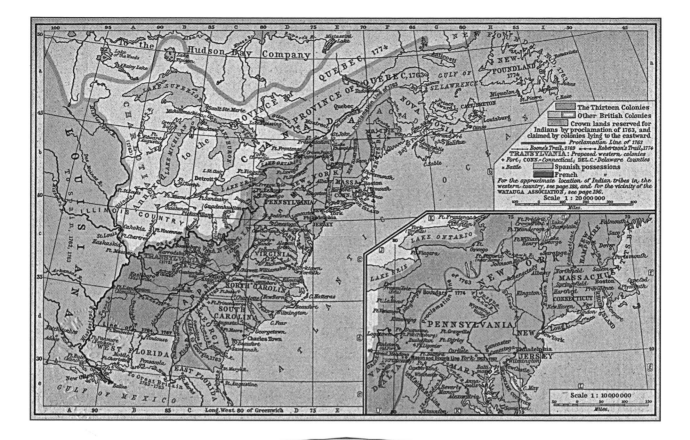

The thirteen original colonies, which later became the start of the United States of America, are shown on this map of North America from 1763–1775. All of the colonies were founded by the British, with the exception of New York (originally settled by the Dutch) and Delaware (by Sweden). But eventually they, too, fell under British rule. Miles away from England, and often ignored, the American colonies established local institutions of government. Fed up with their treatment by England, specifically with trade restrictions and heavy taxation, the colonies joined together to form their own union.

"English" as the other colonial cities. Many varieties of Europeans and free Africans settled there.

Virginia, the Carolinas, and Georgia made up the sparsely populated southern colonies. The South was quite prosperous, with large rice and tobacco plantations along the rivers. The port city of Charleston, South Carolina, was the largest city in the South and was well known as a center of English culture.

The thirteen American colonies were linked by a shared language and history, but little else. Each colony had been established by a charter and had decided on its own form of government. Some were proprietary colonies, meaning they were owned and managed by English businesses. Others were royal colonies headed by a governor appointed by the king. Some New England colonies were self-governing from the beginning.

English settlers brought with them two important political ideas. The first was that people can create their own governments and the second was that people have a right to govern themselves. Settlers in Spanish or French colonies did not question the right of kings to make unpopular laws, and they did not have a tradition of voting for public officials. All the English colonies had legislatures (governing bodies responsible for passing and enforcing laws). Some legislators were elected; others were appointed.

Some English settlers came to America because they wanted the freedom to live and worship as they pleased. Most came for economic opportunities. These settlers put a high value on education. They felt that if all citizens could read, write, and think for themselves, they could participate in government. In most of Europe, only the very wealthy were educated, and the nobility controlled local government.

Not all people in the English colonies could participate in government. Only white men who owned property were allowed to vote or to seek office. In some colonies, voters also had to be members of the accepted Protestant church. Many of these men thought of voting as their "natural right," but they did not consider allowing Native Americans, African Americans, or women to participate in government. Nor did they discuss freeing the slaves.

For 150 years after the first permanent settlement in Jamestown, Virginia, in 1607, colonists did not think of uniting the colonies into one nation or of cutting their ties to England. The kings did not interfere in their lives, and colonists were content with rule under Parliament, England's governing body. Then, in 1763, everything began to change.

TIMELINE

1763 — War between England and France (French and Indian War) ends.

1764 — Colonists react to a tax on sugar with a boycott.

1765 — Parliament passes the Stamp Act, angering colonists who declare "no taxation without representation." The Quartering Act allows British troops to be housed in American homes. The Sons of Liberty is organized to oppose British laws.

1767 — Parliament passes the Townshend Acts, taxes on glass, lead, paint, paper, and tea; Samuel Adams writes letters of protest that circulate in the colonies.

1772 — Committees of Correspondence continue the letter-writing campaign.

1773 — The Boston Tea Party destroys British property.

1774 — Parliament passes the Coercive Acts, or the Intolerable Acts, and orders the port of Boston closed. The First Continental Congress meets in Philadelphia and sends a Declaration of

TIMELINE

Rights and Grievances to George III. Minutemen are organized in New England.

1775 — War with Britain begins. The Second Continental Congress convenes in Philadelphia.

1776 — The Declaration of Independence ends colonial allegiance to Great Britain.

1777 — Congress adopts the Articles of Confederation.

1781 — The Articles of Confederation are ratified. Cornwallis surrenders to Washington at Yorktown, Virginia.

1782 — The Treaty of Paris ends the war between Great Britain and the United States.

1787 — The U.S. Constitution is written to take the place of the ineffective Articles of Confederation.

1789 — George Washington takes office as the first president of the United States.

CHAPTER 1

In 1763, the American colonies and Great Britain were at peace. Twelve years later they were at the brink of war. How did the relationship between them change so quickly? The reasons were both economic and political.

Economy

From England's point of view, its relationship with the colonies was an economic one. Colonies were an essential part of England's mercantile system. Under mercantilism, colonies were established for one reason: to serve the mother country. The American colonies supplied raw material, such as lumber, to England for manufacture there, and they were a market for English-made goods. By law, the colonies were not allowed to manufacture goods that could be made in England, and they could buy only English-made goods. Colonial business owners were not allowed to trade with other countries on their own. American crops, especially tobacco, rice, and indigo, could be exported only to England or to another English colony. These laws limited America's growth.

"TAXATION WITHOUT REPRESENTATION IS TYRANNY!"

Boston

The American colonies served as rich financial resources for England. The fertile land of the southern colonies allowed Britain to trade rice and tobacco. Shipbuilding also proved to be profitable. The illustration above portrays a variety of work done in the colonies. In the foreground, men chop, pack, and mill. Behind them, farmers plow fields. And in the background, ships in the harbor leave the port full of goods to sell to other countries.

Trade—exporting and importing goods—was the major source of revenue for the American colonies, and their welfare depended on it. The port cities of Boston and Charleston were full of activity, with ships arriving weekly to be unloaded and loaded. England regulated trade with all of its colonies in Asia and Africa, as well as in America, through the Navigation Acts. One law specified that goods imported or exported by English colonies had to be shipped on English-made ships by English crews. ("English" included Americans.) By 1760, nearly half of the English ships were American-built, and shipbuilding was a profitable industry.

Mercantilism was considered a good system because it ensured markets for both England and its colonies, but it did not allow the colonies to expand independently of the mother country.

Politics

The American colonies and Great Britain were separated by the Atlantic Ocean. Communication between the two was very slow because it took several weeks to cross the Atlantic by ship. It was easy for years to go by without conflict. As long as trade was profitable, the English Parliament was not concerned about what English subjects in the colonies were doing.

French colonists were another matter. From the beginning years of English settlement, France and England fought for control of the North American continent. In 1754, a war began between the French and their Indian allies, and the English. In 1763, France surrendered and England took over Canada and the West Indies.

The French and Indian War was expensive. The English Parliament decided to pay its bills by taxing the colonies. It also decided to keep 10,000 British troops, called redcoats, in the colonies to make certain that the French did not return. Both decisions were very unpopular in America.

For the next ten years, a series of tax acts infuriated the colonists, who saw no reason to pay England's debts when they had had no say about them. "Taxation without representation is tyranny!" they shouted. They felt they were being ruled by a cruel dictatorship. When they refused to pay the taxes or boycotted (refused to buy) English products, Parliament reacted by passing even harsher laws to punish the rebels.

Beginning in the 1770s, the ideas of a few men—Samuel Adams, James Otis, John Dickinson, and Patrick Henry among

The Stamp Act of 1765, shown here and now housed in the Library of Congress, was one way England planned on paying its debts from the French and Indian War. The act stated that all important documents, journals, pamphlets, and playing cards be marked with stamps purchased from the British government. Irked by Britain's thoughtless demands, the colonists revolted by mobbing ships carrying stamped papers. They disregarded the law and banned English goods as well. This resistance, as well as the interference on the part of sympathetic lawmakers and merchants, resulted in the repeal of the Stamp Act in March 1766. However, England also established supreme power over the colonies, which angered the colonists and led to the American Revolution.

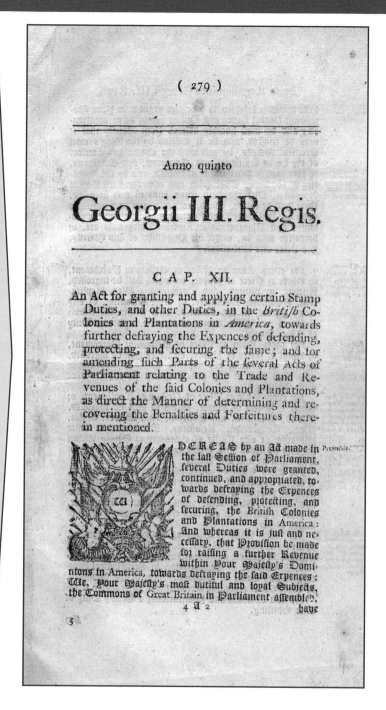

others—were heard throughout the colonies. They questioned the right of England to rule America so harshly. They insisted that their own rights be respected. A group in Massachusetts formed the Sons of Liberty to oppose these taxes by any means they could. Women and girls organized the Daughters of Liberty.

Boston Tea Party, by W. D. Cooper, depicts American colonists in Boston throwing tea cargo off British ships. To protest an imposed tax on tea about which they had no say, a group of Bostonians disguised as Indians boarded ships and dumped 342 chests of tea into Boston Harbor. In retaliation, Britain passed the Coercive Acts, also known as the Intolerable Acts, which were meant to keep the colonies in line. Instead, it compelled them to unite and stand up to their mother country.

They spun their own thread on spinning wheels to avoid buying British-made cloth, clearly breaking the law.

As hated as the taxes were, even worse was the threat of the Quartering Act. Parliament had decreed that British soldiers could be housed with colonists against their will, intimidating them and invading their privacy.

Gradually, many colonists came to see that they were together in their opposition to hateful English laws and an unsympathetic Parliament. They realized they had more in common with each other than geography. They formed Committees of Correspondence to send letters to like-minded people to let each other know what was going on in their colony and how angry they felt about it. Express riders (Paul Revere was the best known) took these messages from one town to another.

For some, letter writing was not enough. Colonial leaders wanted to meet with each other in person to confer about their problems with Great Britain. The Stamp Act of 1765 gave them their first opportunity. The Stamp Act required that all paper—legal documents, licenses, contracts, newspapers, pamphlets, and even playing cards—carry a stamp paid for by a tax. Outraged colonists called for a "congress" to discuss the issue. At that time, a congress simply meant a conference. It was not a governing body, but a group of men coming together to share their ideas. They hoped that their meeting would get the sympathetic attention of the Crown.

It had the opposite effect. Parliament refused to recognize that a colonial congress had any authority and continued to pass new taxes. In response to a new tax on tea in December 1773, Boston patriots stole onboard British ships in the harbor and dumped cases of tea into the water. As punishment for the "tea party," Parliament closed the port of Boston to all shipping. The Massachusetts legislature, supported by those in Rhode Island and Virginia, declared this act "intolerable." Patriots prepared to fight back with muskets.

But before they rushed to war, colonial leaders called for another meeting, a Continental Congress. Some colonies elected delegates to the congress openly; others appointed them secretly. Some delegates were loyal to the king; some were not; all of them cared very much about the future of America.

CHAPTER 2

THE FIRST CONTINENTAL CONGRESS

In the first days of September 1774, about fifty delegates from twelve colonies (Georgia did not participate, although it was invited) gathered in Philadelphia with feelings of uncertainty, excitement, and hope. Delegates found Philadelphia's hospitality warm. John Adams called it a "city of feasts" because of the great number of dinner parties delegates were invited to.

"This is a young, smart, spirited body," Adams wrote in his diary about the men he met. Silas Deane of Connecticut confided to his wife on September 1, "We are in high spirits." Joseph Galloway of Pennsylvania was a little more cautious. He wrote to the governor of New Jersey in early September, "I think [the Congress] will behave with Temper and Moderation."

The First Continental Congress met at Carpenters' Hall in Philadelphia, Pennsylvania, on September 5, 1774, as shown in this painting by Clyde DeLand. Fifty-six delegates from the thirteen colonies participated. Because they could be persecuted for treason if they were found out, the Congress met in secret to discuss their conflict with England. After vetoing the idea of continuing to live under British rule but demanding more freedom, the Congress voted for a declaration of rights.

King George III (1738–1820) incited the American Revolution by refusing to give in to any of the colonies' demands. After emerging victorious from the French and Indian War with France, George insisted on taxing the colonies to recoup war debts. Even as the colonists were winning the Revolution, George stubbornly continued until America had won its independence. Suffering from a disease called porphyria, George's rule was interrupted by compromised health, and he died blind, deaf, and mad.

It was expected that the meeting would be short. Colonial legislatures had instructed the delegates what to do. For instance, New Hampshire delegates were told to:

> devise, consult, and adopt measures, as may have the most likely tendency to extricate the Colonies from their present difficulties; to secure and perpetuate their rights, liberties, and privileges, and to restore that peace, harmony, and mutual confidence which once happily subsisted between the parent country and her Colonies.

The majority of delegates wanted to restore peace between the colonies and England, not to declare their independence from the Crown. However, they also wanted to preserve their rights, even if that meant war. Most were confident that once King George III heard how unhappy the colonists were, he would repeal the hateful laws. A few radicals from Massachusetts and Virginia muttered about political freedom, but did so very quietly.

Delegates

The first order of business was getting to know each other. Although the delegates knew of each other by reputation and through the Committees of Correspondence, most had never met because travel between the colonies was so difficult. They carried with them the opinions of their friends and neighbors and intended to protect the interests of their own neighborhoods and their own colonies.

Many of the men who served during the First or Second Continental Congress have since become familiar to Americans as the Founding Fathers: John Adams, Benjamin Franklin, Thomas Jefferson, John Hancock, and Richard Henry Lee, for instance. But most of the 300 delegates that served over the Continental Congress's fourteen-year history are not well known today.

Among the first delegates were twenty-five lawyers, twelve merchants, four physicians, two farmers, nine landowners, and one minister. One half of the men were college graduates, which was remarkable for that time.

Payton Randolph, the speaker of Virginia's House of Burgesses (America's first representative legislature), was unanimously elected presiding officer at the first Congress. There would be thirteen presidents after him. Charles Thompson of Philadelphia was named secretary. Thompson served as secretary until the Congress was dissolved in 1789, faithfully taking notes at each session, copying petitions, and writing letters, all in longhand with a quill pen. Everything was carefully saved, and when the papers of the Continental Congress were collected, they made up 170,000 manuscript pages.

Delegates adopted a rule of secrecy that was closely followed. This allowed them to speak their minds freely without fear of arrest. Until independence was accepted by England, they were considered traitors and could have been arrested and taken to England for trial.

Purpose

The Congress had to invent itself. It was a new organization and the delegates had to decide its purpose. Was it to advise the colonies only? Could it take action? Could it make binding laws? Must all delegates agree on a proposal or would the majority rule? Were they to follow parliamentary procedure or make their own?

If they voted by colony, instead of as individual delegates, would each colony have the same number of votes or should votes be allocated on the basis of population, or trade revenue, or geographic size of the colony?

Patrick Henry reminded the gathering that this was the first general congress in the 150 years of colonial history, and they had to make their own rules. They should not act as the English Parliament did, because conditions in America were much different than those in England.

Henry urged the delegates to think nationally. John Adams recorded in his diary on September 5 that Henry had declared, "The distinctions between Virginia, New York, and New England are no more. I am not a Virginian, but an American." Henry's words were very influential and started delegates thinking of themselves as "American," too, rather than as New Yorkers or Pennsylvanians.

Colonists were most concerned with their rights and how they were being violated. They felt they had the same rights as all Englishmen, based on the British constitution and the colonial charters. "Emigrants do not leave their allegiances when they leave their native land," Richard Henry Lee of Virginia argued, according to John Adams. He believed they should still be citizens of their native land no matter where they lived.

After a few weeks of discussion, one committee was formed to list the colonists' rights and another to list their grievances (complaints) to send to the king. They then combined the lists into a Declaration of Rights and Grievances. The declaration began with the recap of the events of the past ten years, since the end of the French and Indian War, emphasizing the unpopular laws passed, "all of which are impolitic [unwise], unjust, and cruel, as well as unconstitutional, and most dangerous and destructive of American rights." They pointed out that when earlier complaints were made, they were "repeatedly treated with contempt by His Majesty's ministers of state." The petition continued:

> [O]ur ancestors, who first settled these colonies, were at the time of their emigration from the mother country, entitled to all the rights, liberties, and immunities of free and natural born subjects within the realm of England . . .
>
> That the foundation of English liberty, and of all free government, is a right in the people to participate in their legislative council . . . they are entitled to a free and exclusive power of legislation . . .
>
> In the course of our inquiry, we find many infringements and violations of the foregoing rights, which, from an ardent desire that harmony and mutual intercourse of affection and

This is the first page of the Petition of the First Continental Congress to King George. It was handwritten by John Dickinson on October 26, 1774, and is now housed in the Library of Congress. The petition was meant to be a respectful letter to air the colonists' complaints. It read, in part, "in behalf of ourselves and the inhabitants of those colonies that have deputed us to represent them in General Congress, by this our humble petition, beg leave to lay our grievances before the throne."

interest may be restored . . . to state such acts and measures as have been adopted since the last war which demonstrate a system formed to enslave America.

They then listed their major grievances: taxation without representation; closing the port of Boston; and keeping a standing army in several colonies. They explained that they planned to form an association to boycott British goods and to stop exporting American ones to Britain. They would also sign a "non-consumption" agreement, refusing to use any British goods already in the colonies.

The Declaration of Rights and Grievances was sent to King George III on October 24, 1774. The delegates went home with the hope that the king would instruct Parliament to make changes in the laws affecting the colonies. Peace would be restored and life would go on as usual. They planned to meet again in Philadelphia in the spring, on May 10, 1775, to hear the king's response.

CHAPTER 3

King George III did not respond to the Declaration of Rights and Grievances himself. Instead, he gave the document to his colonial agents. Ignoring the petition was the worst thing he could do because it ended all traces of loyalty among the delegates. At the same time, the English Parliament passed a law to stop trade between New England and the other colonies. If they obeyed the law, their economy would suffer. New Englanders refused to obey.

THE SECOND CONTINENTAL CONGRESS

In 1774, edgy Massachusetts patriots had formed groups of militia called minutemen. These "instant soldiers" promised to fight the red-coated British soldiers with a moment's notice. Now they were primed and ready.

On April 19, 1775, just before the second Congress gathered, British troops marched toward Concord, Massachusetts, to get the ammunition they had stored there. Express riders Paul Revere and William Dawes alerted the countryside and the minutemen assembled. As the Americans marched toward Lexington, they encountered British troops. The first shot was fired—no one is sure by whom—and the Revolutionary War (1775-1783) began.

All across the colonies, residents got ready for conflict, building arsenals of weapons. In early May, a ragtag group of soldiers called

The American Revolution began with the Battle of Lexington and Concord on April 19, 1775. The fight on Lexington Common is depicted above in an oil painting by Howard Pyle. As British redcoats met up with American militiamen, a shot was fired, prompting the British to kill eight Americans and wound ten others. The fighting moved on to Concord, where the Americans were more prepared.

the Green Mountain Boys marched to the British-held Fort Ticonderoga in northern New York. They took the undermanned fort easily and captured cannons that they dragged back to Massachusetts for the defense of Boston. More cannons and ammunition were captured at the British garrison at Crown Point a little farther north on Lake Champlain. Militia groups formed in other colonies and looked for opportunities to capture weapons.

The Congress Responds

As the delegates listened to the responses of the king's agents in May 1775, they were aware of the rebellion that seethed around them. They also understood that no changes would be made in their favor. The king would continue to ignore their grievances, and Parliament would continue to make laws without asking for their input.

Deciding what to do about the situation seemed to take an unnecessarily long time because the Congress had agreed that each delegate not only had a right to speak on each issue, but had a duty to do so as well. Each man had opinions on the regulations governing trade, personal liberty, loyalty, and the power of the Congress to make laws and wage a war. All delegates received a steady stream of letters and newspapers from home. The delegates felt they were representing these constituents, so they read their letters carefully and repeated their ideas during the long discussions. This procedure became the basis of representative democracy: the insistence that all opinions matter, and that elected officials must consider the opinions of voters.

For an impatient and impulsive man like John Adams, the wait was frustrating. He wrote to a friend on May 21, 1775, "Our unwieldy body moves very slow. We shall do something in Time, but must have our own Way."

Although most of the delegates realized a break with England was impossible to avoid, some insisted that they try to reach the king one more time before they initiated a full-scale war. In July 1775, John Dickinson of Pennsylvania wrote an "Olive Branch" petition, asking the king to repeal the hated laws. The petition stated that it would be necessary to resort to arms to get the king's attention but promised that the fighting would end as soon as the British government met their demands.

King George ignored the petition. In August 1775, he issued a proclamation declaring the colonies to be in a state of rebellion. He

The Olive Branch Petition was signed on July 8, 1775, by forty-eight members of the Continental Congress. Representatives from all of the original colonies but Rhode Island gave King George one last chance to avoid a war for independence. Unfortunately for the fate of England, the king ignored the petition, declaring in a speech to Parliament on October 26, 1775, "It is now become the part of wisdom . . . to put a speedy end to these disorders by the most decisive exertions." The document shown above is the working copy of the petition and was sent separately to Lord Dartmouth, secretary of state for the colonies, in England. See transcription on page 55.

ordered his officers and loyal subjects to suppress the revolt "and bring the traitors to justice," as he wrote. From his point of view, American "patriots" were traitors and should be jailed or executed.

It was clear to the delegates by then that they must formally unite in their opposition to the king. They talked for hours about how they could forge thirteen individual colonies into one nation. Other than hatred for oppression, what did they have in common? It was necessary that they find common ground before going forward.

They knew they had to defend themselves first. Many British soldiers were already in America and others were on their way over. Without a colonial army and navy, the British would take over by force. Members of the Continental Congress would be arrested and sent to England for trial.

In mid-June 1775, John Adams proposed that a Continental army be raised. The Congress unanimously selected George Washington to be the commander in chief. The Virginian had impressed all the delegates with his quiet determination and courage. In the early days of the conflict, Adams reported that Washington had said, "I will raise one thousand men, subsist them at my own expense, and march myself at their head for the relief of Boston."

Six months after an army of 15,000 men was established, a navy was authorized. Because there wasn't time to build warships, Congress authorized privateering—taking over private ships and converting them into warships. The new navy was instructed to capture English ships in the West Indies and bring the cargo back to the United States. If the cargo was rum, it could be sold and the money given to Congress; a cargo of guns could be used by the army.

This engraving after a work by Julian Scott was published in the magazine *Harper's Weekly* in 1877. It depicts the Continental army at Valley Forge, Pennsylvania. General George Washington made Valley Forge his headquarters during the winter of 1777–1778. The location was chosen because of its proximity to both the British army in Philadelphia and the Continental Congress, in York, Pennsylvania, at that time. The brutal winter took its toll on America's troops, but with rigorous military training throughout the winter, they emerged as a force to be reckoned with.

To raise money for the war, Congress approved issuing paper money without gold to back it up, something it would later regret.

With the framework for fighting a war in place, the delegates turned their minds to the most pressing issue of all: Should they make an official break from England?

CHAPTER 4

The debate over declaring formal independence from Great Britain continued through the winter and spring of 1776. Arguments frequently became heated. Many colonists could not imagine a life without England in control, and they distrusted the plans being made. Others thought that life in America was possible only without British control. Echoes of Patrick Henry's famous speech came to mind: "Give me liberty or give me death."

THE DECLARATION OF INDEPENDENCE

On March 20, Joseph Hewes of North Carolina wrote, "We do not treat each other with that decency and respect that was observed heretofore. Jealousies, ill-natured observations and recriminations take the place of reason and argument. Our Tempers are soured."

A month later, Samuel Adams of Massachusetts wrote that he was still hearing of the need for reconciliation with England,

Clyde DeLand painted this 1915 scene of Patrick Henry delivering his famous speech to the second Virginia Convention on March 23, 1775. Radically opposed to the British government, Henry used his exceptional gifts as a public speaker to convince the delegates of the Continental Congress that independence from England was the best solution. The words he spoke have become some of the most famous in American history: "I know not what course others may take, but as for me, give me liberty or give me death."

"I am exceedingly disgusted when I hear it mentioned . . . The only Alternative is Independency or Slavery."

James Duane of New York and James Wilson of Pennsylvania spoke against a break with England at this time. They believed there was no rush, even if it was inevitable. The colonies weren't ready for independence. "Before we are prepared to build the new house, why should we pull down the old one, and expose ourselves to all the inclemencies [severity] of the season?" they wrote.

There were many other questions to be answered, from how to create a post office to deliver mail to how to raise money for running this new government without taxes. What kind of national offices would be needed? Without a structure of royalty, as there was in England, how would a hierarchy of importance be achieved? How would a judiciary system be developed? And how would they establish relations with other nations?

Others felt it was more important to achieve independence first; the details could come later. Months went by with much talk and no action.

The Resolution

The colonial legislatures moved faster on the issue than the national body did. In April 1776, the North Carolina legislature authorized its delegation to vote for independence. The next month the Virginia House of Burgesses forced the question by passing a resolution that the Continental Congress vote on independence immediately. The resolution sat for several days on the desk of Virginia's delegate, Richard Henry Lee, while he decided how and when to introduce it.

Massachusetts delegate Samuel Adams wrote to a friend on June 6, "Tomorrow a motion will be made, and a Question I hope decided, the most important that was ever agitated in America." The next day, Lee introduced a resolution urging the Congress to declare its independence from Great Britain. It was worded simply:

> That these United Colonies are, and of right ought to be, free and independent States, that they are absolved from all allegiance to the British Crown, and that all political connection between them and the State of Great Britain is, and ought to be, totally dissolved.
>
> That it is expedient forthwith to take the most effectual measures for forming foreign Alliances.
>
> That a plan of confederation be prepared and transmitted to the respective Colonies for their consideration and approbation.

There was no certainty the resolution would pass. On June 8, South Carolina delegate Edward Rutledge wrote to John Jay of New York. "The Congress sat till 8 o'clock this evening in consequence of a motion of R. H. Lee rendering ourselves free and independent State. The sensible part of the House opposed the Motion . . . they saw no Wisdom in a Declaration of Independence," which would alert Great Britain to such a plan.

The thoughtful Jefferson wrote later in his "Account of a Declaration" that he was very nervous about the vote. "The people of the middle colonies (Maryland, Delaware, Pennsylvania, New Jersey, and New York) were not ripe for bidding adieu to British connection . . ." The middle colonies, as well as South Carolina, benefited the most from the mercantile system and considered themselves far removed from the problems in New England.

"Congress never were so much engaged as at this time," wrote William Whipple of New Hampshire on June 10. "[B]usiness presses on them exceedingly . . . There are so many irons in the fire, I fear some of them will burn."

The best argument for declaring independence was the need to create alliances with other nations, particularly France, for help against the British army. If they remained British colonies, they could not expect to find support anywhere in Europe.

Congressional leaders felt that all the colonies had to agree to independence. Just one colony against independence might give aid to the enemy, and the war would be lost. Most of those who voted "nay" in the early votes did not oppose the idea of separation from Great Britain, but they didn't want a declaration made until all the colonies supported it fully.

The Declaration

On June 11, 1776, Congress appointed a committee to begin preparing a formal declaration in case the votes changed. Thomas Jefferson, John Adams, Benjamin Franklin, Roger Sherman, and Robert Livingston were appointed to draft the document.

Meanwhile, another committee was appointed to draw up the Articles of Confederation, the second part of Lee's resolution, to organize the operation of the new government. Thus when one government was dissolved, another would be ready to take its place. On June 17, the name of the confederation was proposed and accepted. The new nation would be known as the United States of America.

This document fragment is from the earliest known draft of the Declaration of Independence. Handwritten by Thomas Jefferson in June 1776, this draft shows that Jefferson heavily edited his first attempt at the famous document before handing over a cleaner copy that we know as the original rough draft. The writing on the bottom half of the page is Jefferson's draft of a resolution on the resignation of General John Sullivan.

As the time to vote on the independence resolution neared, John Adams wrote, "We are now in the very midst of a revolution, the most completely unexpected, and remarkable of any in the history of nations." Most likely, the other delegates agreed with him.

"I expect the grand question will be determined in Congress [on June 28]," William Whipple wrote, "that being the day assigned to receive the report of a Committee who are preparing the Declaration."

On that day, the draft of the Declaration of Independence was read to the Congress. It began with a preamble:

When in the Course of human events it becomes necessary for one people to dissolve the political bonds which have connected them with another, and assume among the powers of the earth, the separate and equal station to which the Laws of Nature and Nature's God entitle them, a decent respect to the opinions of mankind requires that they should declare the causes which impel them to the separation.

We hold these truths to be self-evident, that all men are created equal, that they are endowed by their Creator with certain inalienable Rights, that among these are Life, Liberty and the pursuit of Happiness.—That to secure these rights, Governments are instituted among Men, deriving their just powers from the consent of the governed.—That whenever any Form of Government becomes destructive of these ends, it is the Right of the People to alter or to abolish it, and to institute new Government, laying its foundation on such principles . . .

The First Public Reading of the Declaration of Independence, a lithograph by Howard Pyle, was published in 1880 in *Harper's Weekly*. Pennsylvania militia colonel John Nixon administered the first public reading of the Declaration of Independence in a crowded town square.

Then followed a restatement of the grievances the colonies had suffered, but there was now no hint of reconciliation. They were simply listed as reasons for dissolving the bonds between the two nations. As the delegates listened to the declaration, they made notes about what to add, cut, or rewrite. Then the document went back to the committee for revision.

The Vote

Two votes were necessary to make independence from England official. One vote was on Lee's resolution to end allegiance to the British Crown; the other was to accept the

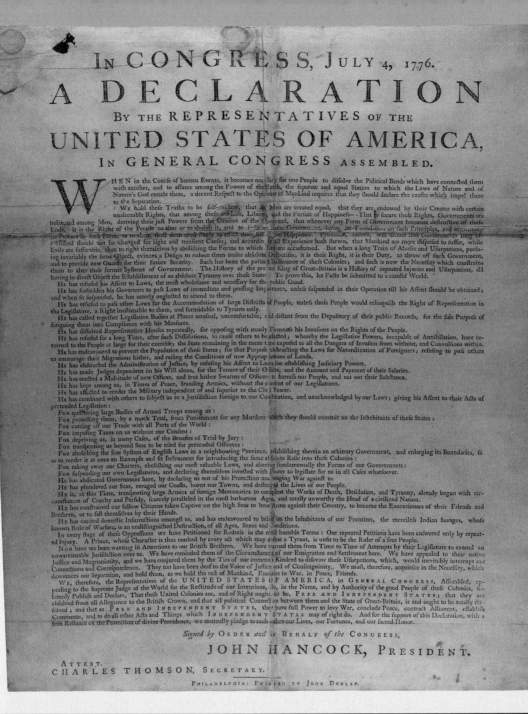

Once the Declaration of Independence was completed and adopted, the Continental Congress ordered it be printed. A Philadelphia printer named John Dunlap produced the first printed text of the declaration, which is now known as the Dunlap Broadside, on July 4, 1776. These broadsides were distributed to political and military leaders. Only twenty-four Dunlap Broadsides still exist. The officially inscribed copy of the Declaration of Independence, copied in a large hand and featuring John Hancock's famous bold signature, was ordered on July 19, 1776. That document is on permanent display at the National Archives. See transcription excerpt on page 56.

written Declaration of Independence. Congress had decided that each colony (rather than each delegate) would have one vote. Within each colonial delegation of three to five members, individuals might vote against the measure, but the majority had to accept it for their "yea" vote to count. Unless all the colonies voted for it, the issue would be dropped.

The vote on the independence resolution came on July 2, 1776. Nine colonies had promised to vote for it: New Hampshire, Connecticut, Massachusetts, Rhode Island, New Jersey, Maryland, Virginia, North Carolina, and Georgia. New York and Pennsylvania were waiting for instructions from their state legislators and would not vote. South Carolina was against the resolution, but agreed to vote for it if all the other colonies did.

Delaware had a three-man delegation. One man was for, the other was against, and the third was absent. To break the tie and ensure that Delaware's vote would be for independence, absent delegate Caesar Rodney rode all night, arriving in Philadelphia just in time to cast his vote. The colonies were united on the vote for the resolution with no "nays" being recorded. Delegate Robert Treat Paine of Massachusetts noted in his diary on July 2, "The Independence of the State Voted and declared."

On July 4, the Congress voted to accept the wording of Jefferson's declaration without discussion or celebration from the weary delegates. John Adams wrote to his wife, Abigail, "If it had been made seven months ago, it would have been attended with many great and glorious efforts."

By July 5, copies of the Declaration of Independence were being distributed in New Jersey and Delaware. On July 6, the *Pennsylvania Evening Post* printed it in full. On July 9, General Washington ordered the Declaration of Independence read to the American army. As word of the declaration spread, colonists cheered, lit bonfires (sometimes burning British goods), and rang church bells.

Delegates gathered in Philadelphia on August 2, 1776, to sign the document. The Declaration of Independence closed with the ringing words, "We mutually pledge to each other our lives, our fortunes, and our sacred honor." The signers knew that if their struggle for independence failed, their property would be confiscated and they could be executed. Indeed, over the course of the war, five were arrested (including three of the four signers from South Carolina), ten lost their homes, and seventeen lost other property. The war years ahead would be very difficult for all the colonists, but no one suggested giving in.

CHAPTER 5

Once the excitement of declaring independence was over, the hard work of winning it began.

In 1775, when the war began in Massachusetts, the Continental army wasn't an army. It was a group of boys and men who came together to keep British soldiers from taking over their farms and houses. They were not prepared to leave their work and families to fight a long war. They had had no military training and were given no uniforms, and the only weapons they carried were the ones they brought from home. No camps or forts had been established for them, and they slept on the ground or in barns when they were on the march. They found food when and where they could.

CONGRESS WAGES WAR

Few of the officers had been tested in battle. George Washington was an exception. He had served in the British army during the French and Indian War and knew how to lead men. Congress chose most of the officers from volunteers and from the recommendations of others. Disappointment and disaster was the frequent result. Many officers didn't know how to plan battles, organize camps, or command soldiers.

Oliver Wolcott of Connecticut lamented on March 22, 1777, that if the colonies had had a "Regular army . . . we probably should have been able to have crushed the British Power in America." But the army was far from "regular." Poorly trained town militia, colonial troops, and frontier sharpshooters were in the field with the Continental army.

Congress passed a law requiring each colony to recruit a certain number of men for the colonial army, but it was hard to enforce. John Adams wrote that these quotas were impossible to fill because "some colonies have such bodies of Quakers, and Mennonites, and Moravians, who are principled against War, and other have such Bodies of Tories [loyal to Britain], or Cowards, or unprincipled People who will not wage War." He didn't mention that men were reluctant to sign up because they would have to leave their work and families and might not get paid to risk their lives.

The day after independence was declared, Joseph Hews of North Carolina wrote, "We resolve to raise regiments, resolve to make Cannon, resolve to make and import muskets, powder, and clothing, but it is a melancholy fact that near half of our men, Cannon, muskets, powder, clothes, etc., is to be found nowhere but on paper."

Finding supplies was just as hard as finding men. Congress asked the colonies for supplies first, and when that didn't work, it tried to buy or borrow them, and as a last resort, took them. Farmers were required to give a percentage of their crops to feed soldiers. Horses were frequently requisitioned for the troops.

The British knew how important supplies were and went after colonial storerooms. In May 1777, they destroyed 1,700 barrels of salted meat and 1,000 barrels of flour, a devastating loss to the new army. "Powder! Powder!" was the never-ending call from the front lines where unarmed soldiers were useless.

John Hancock and Charles Thomson signed the document shown above, appointing George Washington to the position of commander in chief of the Continental army. The commission dates from June 19, 1775, and is housed in the Library of Congress. Washington was chosen because of his military experience. Although he was reluctant to accept the post, the army won independence for the colonies.

Congress hoped that Canada would join the colonies in the rebellion, adding needed manpower and supplies. They were disappointed to find that most Canadians wanted to remain loyal to England. Even worse, Americans loyal to the Crown (Tories) flocked to Canada, seeking safety from angry rebels. According to Edmund C. Burnett's book, *The Continental Congress,* John Adams said of English sympathizers: "A Tory here is the most despicable animal in the creation. Spiders, toads, snakes are their only proper emblems."

During the six years of war, the Continental Congress had to move its meeting place frequently to keep out of the line of fire from the advancing British army. It went from

Philadelphia to Baltimore, to York and Lancaster, Pennsylvania, to Princeton, New Jersey, and Annapolis, Maryland, before returning to Philadelphia.

Daily dispatches kept Congress, wherever it was, informed of the military campaigns. Rumors ran through Congress, and sometimes members had to wait days to learn the truth. News from the front kept members alternating between despair and elation. They were constantly distressed over the high number of deserters and the terrible conditions at camps like Valley Forge.

Several congressional committees were created to oversee the administration of the war. There were so many committees that delegates had to serve on several at once. Paperwork took up much of their time and they complained of being so busy with small matters, they could not attend to the large ones. They spent their days writing and reading letters and reports, and dealing with resignations, promotions, desertions, court-martials, and other disciplinary measures.

The medical department of Congress had to find ways to keep the soldiers as healthy as possible. Smallpox, dysentery, influenza, and other infections killed thousands of men. Little effective medicine was available. The lack of decent food or housing, exhaustion, and cold killed many, as well. Unheated barns were converted into hospitals, and no nursing care was available.

Paying for War

Finding the money to pay for a government was always a challenge for Congress. At that time, silver or gold coins (specie) were used for most financial transactions. Bills of credit were issued for large purchases and then paid off in specie. Congress estimated the cost of the war at 5 million dollars, an impossibly large sum

These two images—the front and back of a five dollar bill—are examples of the currency that the Continental Congress had printed to cover the cost of the war. Continentals, as they were called, became worthless almost immediately because there was no gold or silver to back them up. They were investments in the future of America, backed by the hope of future tax monies, and would be redeemable only when the colonies broke from England. Issuing Continentals was another way America declared its independence. It was the first time money used by the colonies wasn't marked with the faces of European royalty. In 1785 the Continental Congress adopted the dollar as the unit for national currency. "Not worth a Continental" became a popular expression to describe something that lacked value.

then. America did not have enough specie to pay for a war, so Congress issued bills of credit and authorized the printing of paper money without gold or silver to back it up.

The paper money, called Continentals, became almost worthless. In January of 1777, when it was first issued, $1.25 in paper money was worth $1.00 in silver or gold. Five years later, it took $167.50 in paper money to buy a dollar's worth of specie. Gradually the worthless money was taken out of circulation.

Congress then did not have the power to tax, so it asked for contributions from the states. Most states planned to use what money they had for their own needs and were unable or unwilling to pay the nation's debts. In 1781, the nation was almost bankrupt and Congress suspended all payments. Soldiers who hadn't been paid for months were near mutiny. It was only their high regard for General Washington that kept them in the field.

Foreign Relations

Congress wanted the new nation to be recognized by Europe. In the early years, the Committee of Secret Correspondence was responsible for dealing with European leaders, trying to make alliances and find financial support. Later, the committee was called the Committee on Foreign Affairs and eventually it became the State Department.

During the war, members of Congress were sent to Spain, France, the Netherlands, Austria, and Russia on diplomatic missions. They found the most sympathetic ear in France, England's longtime enemy. In July 1780, 6,000 French soldiers arrived in Rhode Island led by the Marquis de Lafayette. This support, as well as the money France loaned to the United States, was crucial to the nation's victory.

The War Ends

On October 21, 1781, an express rider brought the news to Congress that the British commander, Lord Cornwallis, had surrendered his entire army to General Washington in Yorktown,

The Treaty of Paris of 1783 *(above)* is so named because it was negotiated and signed in Paris, France. John Adams, Benjamin Franklin, and John Jay negotiated with England and other European powers to cement America's independence and to allow for westward expansion. See transcription on pages 56–57.

Virginia. British and American representatives negotiated a peace treaty, the Treaty of Paris, in the fall of 1782 that was finalized on September 3, 1783.

The agreement stated that Great Britain would keep Canada, that those in America who had stayed loyal to England would be protected from revenge, and that English merchants would be paid for old debts. In return, England acknowledged the independence of the United States and agreed to give up its claims to western lands as far as the Mississippi River.

The war had hurt the American economy badly. For six years, all trade had been halted. From Boston fisheries to South Carolina rice fields, the nation had suffered. Now it was time to rebuild.

CHAPTER 6

During the 1780s, the Continental Congress had the tedious work of putting together the American system of government. The excitement of the war was over. The exhilaration of creating a new nation had dimmed. Now there was the day-to-day work of establishing departments and organizing procedures for running the country.

Articles of Confederation

The Articles of Confederation had been adopted by Congress in 1777 and ratified by the states in 1781. The delegates knew there would be problems with the articles before they adopted them, but they were under great pressure to set up some form of government in a hurry. Because of their experience with King George III, most delegates were afraid that a strong central government would turn into a tyranny as bad as the English monarchy. They wanted to be certain their new government would have limited powers. But they limited its powers so much, it became almost powerless.

The articles created a national government with a single house of Congress where each state, regardless of population, had one vote. Small states didn't want to take a chance on being outvoted,

THE END OF THE CONTINENTAL CONGRESS

The Articles of Confederation were adopted by Congress on November 15, 1777. They created an alliance among all of the colonies and named the alliance the United States of America. The document is considered the first constitution of the United States. See transcription excerpt on page 57.

so they insisted this provision be included. Large states thought this was unfair. While there were only thirteen votes in Congress, there were many more delegates, and delegates from the same state rarely agreed on issues, causing many problems in the voting.

There was no chief executive officer (national president) and this meant that Congress had to perform every executive function, an impossible task. It couldn't pass laws and oversee how they were followed.

Congress had few powers that affected the entire nation. It could declare war and negotiate peace; it could raise armed forces; and it could control the development of the western territories. Each state had more power than the national government in regulating commerce and levying taxes. The states could ignore federal laws because they were not enforced.

Nine of the thirteen states had to agree to any federal law Congress might enact before it could become a law, including issuing stamps and minting coins. While Congress could request money from the states, the states had the right to refuse to give it to Congress. Without money, the government could not issue back pay to the soldiers who fought in the war or pay the merchants who had given supplies, food, and ammunition to the army on credit. And until the debts were paid, Congress could make no plans for the future.

Congress was given the authority to mediate disputes between the states, which should have been the job of a judicial system. Listening to petty cases took up much of its time.

Congress could not regulate trade. Each state had its own system of trade regulations, which made trading with the United States very difficult for foreign countries. The port of Charleston had one set of regulations, the port of New York another, and the port of Boston still another.

After five years of trying to govern the nation under the Articles of Confederation, Congress was discouraged. James Manning and Nathan Miller reported to their home state of Rhode Island on September 28, 1786, "It is now agreed by all that our federal Government is but a name; a meer shadow without any substance; and we think it our duty to inform the State that it is totally inefficient for the purposes of the Union . . ."

A New Plan

With the complaints getting louder, several congressmen met in Annapolis, Maryland, in February 1787 to discuss the situation. They decided that instead of trying to modify the articles to make them work, they would start over and write a totally new plan for the government. A Constitutional Convention was held in Philadelphia between May and September of 1787. Under the direction of James Madison, the convention wrote the present United States Constitution. It was ratified the following year.

The new Congress would have two houses, a Senate and a House of Representatives. Two senators would be elected from each state, and representatives were elected based on population. A chief executive officer would be elected through an electoral college, and an independent judiciary would be set up. This is the system used today, and it works so well it has been copied by many other nations.

The Continental Congress met for the last time on October 10, 1788. Its final act was to grant 10 square acres (4.05 hectares) of land just north of Virginia for the creation of a federal town. It would become known as Washington, D.C. Until the new capital city was complete, the new Congress would meet in New York City.

Since all the delegates were not happy with the Articles of Confederation, it was decided that the Congress would start over and draft a new constitution, rather than revise the articles. The new Constitution *(above)* was hammered out by the Constitutional Convention in 1787 and was ratified a year later.

The Continental Congress secretary, Charles Thompson, closed "the Journal of the United States in Congress Assembled" to formally end the session. He then rode on horseback to Mount Vernon, Virginia, and notified George Washington that he had been elected the first president of the United States. Washington would be inaugurated in March 1789.

Americans in 1789 were confident that their new government would bring them peace and prosperity. Through years of debate, trial and error, a war, and economic hard times, they had built a system of representative democracy that would be flexible enough to take them through all the good times and bad that lay ahead of them.

PRIMARY SOURCE TRANSCRIPTIONS

Page 27: Olive Branch Petition of 1775

Transcription Excerpt

July 8, 1775

To the King's Most Excellent Majesty.

The union between our Mother Country and these Colonies, and the energy of mild and just Government, produce benefits so remarkably important, and afforded such an assurance of their permanency and increase, that the wonder and envy of other nations were excited, while they beheld Great Britain rising to a power the most extra-ordinary the world had ever known.

Knowing to what violent resentments and incurable animosities civil discords are apt to exasperate and inflame the contending parties, we think ourselves required by indispensable obligations to Almighty God, to your Majesty, to our fellow-subjects, and to ourselves, immediately to use all the means in our power, not incompatible with our safety, for stopping the further effusion of blood, and for averting the impending calamities that threaten the British Empire.

Attached to your Majesty's person, family, and Government, with all devotion that principle and affection can inspire; connected with Great Britain by the strongest ties that can unite societies, and deploring every event that tends in any degree to weaken thcm, wc solcmnly assure your Majesty, that we not only most ardently desire the former harmony between her and these Colonies may be restored, but that a concord may be established between them upon so firm a basis as to perpetuate its blessings, uninterrupted by any future dissensions.

We therefore beseech your Majesty, that your royal authority and influence may be graciously interposed to procure us relief from our afflicting fears and jealousies, occasioned by the system before-mentioned, and to settle peace through every part of our Dominions, with all humility submitting to your Majesty's wise consideration, whether it may not be expedient, for facilitating those important purposes, that your Majesty be pleased to direct some mode, by which the united applications of your faithful Colonists to the Throne, in pursuance of their common counsels, may be improved into a happy and permanent reconciliation; and that, in the mean time, measures may be taken for preventing the further destruction of the lives of your Majesty's subjects; and that such statutes as more immediately distress any of your Majesty's Colonies may be repealed.

For such arrangements as your Majesty's wisdom can form for collecting the united sense of your American people, we are convinced your Majesty would receive such satisfactory proofs of the disposition of the Colonists towards their Sovereign and Parent State, that the wished for opportunity would soon be restored to them, of evincing the sincerity of their professions, by every testimony of devotion becoming the most dutiful subjects, and the most affectionate Colonists.

Page 38: Declaration of Independence (Dunlap Broadside)

Transcription Excerpt
Declaration of Independence
IN CONGRESS, July 4, 1776.
The unanimous Declaration of the thirteen united States of America,
When in the Course of human events, it becomes necessary for one people to dissolve the political bands which have connected them with another, and to assume among the powers of the earth, the separate and equal station to which the Laws of Nature and of Nature's God entitle them, a decent respect to the opinions of mankind requires that they should declare the causes which impel them to the separation.

We hold these truths to be self-evident, that all men are created equal, that they are endowed by their Creator with certain unalienable Rights, that among these are Life, Liberty and the pursuit of Happiness.—That to secure these rights, Governments are instituted among Men, deriving their just powers from the consent of the governed,—That whenever any Form of Government becomes destructive of these ends, it is the Right of the People to alter or to abolish it, and to institute new Government, laying its foundation on such principles and organizing its powers in such form, as to them shall seem most likely to effect their Safety and Happiness. Prudence, indeed, will dictate that Governments long established should not be changed for light and transient causes; and accordingly all experience hath shewn, that mankind are more disposed to suffer, while evils are sufferable, than to right themselves by abolishing the forms to which they are accustomed. But when a long train of abuses and usurpations, pursuing invariably the same Object evinces a design to reduce them under absolute Despotism, it is their right, it is their duty, to throw off such Government, and to provide new Guards for their future security.—Such has been the patient sufferance of these Colonies; and such is now the necessity which constrains them to alter their former Systems of Government. The history of the present King of Great Britain is a history of repeated injuries and usurpations, all having in direct object the establishment of an absolute Tyranny over these States. To prove this, let Facts be submitted to a candid world.

We, therefore, the Representatives of the united States of America, in General Congress, Assembled, appealing to the Supreme Judge of the world for the rectitude of our intentions, do, in the Name, and by Authority of the good People of these Colonies, solemnly publish and declare, That these United Colonies are, and of Right ought to be Free and Independent States; that they are Absolved from all Allegiance to the British Crown, and that all political connection between them and the State of Great Britain, is and ought to be totally dissolved; and that as Free and Independent States, they have full Power to levy War, conclude Peace, contract Alliances, establish Commerce, and to do all other Acts and Things which Independent States may of right do. And for the support of this Declaration, with a firm reliance on the protection of divine Providence, we mutually pledge to each other our Lives, our Fortunes and our sacred Honor.

Page 47: The Treaty of Paris

Transcription Excerpt
The Definitive Treaty of Peace 1783
In the name of the most holy and undivided Trinity.
It having pleased the Divine Providence to dispose the hearts of the most serene and most potent Prince George the Third, by the grace of God, king of Great Britain, France, and Ireland, defender of the faith, duke of Brunswick and Lunebourg, arch-treasurer and prince elector of the Holy Roman Empire etc., and of the United States of America, to forget all past misunderstandings and differences that have unhappily interrupted the good correspondence and friendship which they mutually wish

to restore, and to establish such a beneficial and satisfactory intercourse, between the two countries upon the ground of reciprocal advantages and mutual convenience as may promote and secure to both perpetual peace and harmony; and having for this desirable end already laid the foundation of peace and reconciliation by the Provisional Articles signed at Paris on the 30th of November 1782, by the commissioners empowered on each part, which articles were agreed to be inserted in and constitute the Treaty of Peace proposed to be concluded between the Crown of Great Britain and the said United States, but which treaty was not to be concluded until terms of peace should be agreed upon between Great Britain and France and his Britannic Majesty should be ready to conclude such treaty accordingly;

Done at Paris, this third day of September in the year of our Lord, one thousand seven hundred and eighty-three.

D. HARTLEY (SEAL)
JOHN ADAMS (SEAL)
B. FRANKLIN (SEAL)
JOHN JAY (SEAL)

Page 50: Articles of Confederation

Transcription Excerpt

Articles of Confederation (1777)
To all to whom these Presents shall come, we the undersigned Delegates of the States affixed to our Names send greeting.

Articles of Confederation and perpetual Union between the states of New Hampshire, Massachusetts-bay Rhode Island and Providence Plantations, Connecticut, New York, New Jersey, Pennsylvania, Delaware, Maryland, Virginia, North Carolina, South Carolina and Georgia.

I. The Stile of this Confederacy shall be "The United States of America."

II. Each state retains its sovereignty, freedom, and independence, and every power, jurisdiction, and right, which is not by this Confederation expressly delegated to the United States, in Congress assembled.

V. For the most convenient management of the general interests of the United States, delegates shall be annually appointed in such manner as the legislatures of each State shall direct, to meet in Congress on the first Monday in November, in every year, with a power reserved to each State to recall its delegates, or any of them, at any time within the year, and to send others in their stead for the remainder of the year.

No State shall be represented in Congress by less than two, nor more than seven members; and no person shall be capable of being a delegate for more than three years in any term of six years; nor shall any person, being a delegate, be capable of holding any office under the United States, for which he, or another for his benefit, receives any salary, fees or emolument of any kind.

Each State shall maintain its own delegates in a meeting of the States, and while they act as members of the committee of the States.

In determining questions in the United States in Congress assembled, each State shall have one vote.

Freedom of speech and debate in Congress shall not be impeached or questioned in any court or place out of Congress, and the members of Congress shall be protected in their persons from arrests or imprisonments, during the time of their going to and from, and attendence on Congress, except for treason, felony, or breach of the peace.

GLOSSARY

allegiance Loyalty.

boycott To refuse to buy a certain product.

confederation A union of states.

constituent A resident of a district represented by an elected official.

delegate A person who is authorized to represent another.

electoral college The body of electors chosen to elect the president and vice president of the United States.

garrison A military post.

judiciary A system of courts of law for the administration of justice.

legislature An organized body in charge of making laws.

mediate To resolve an issue by working with all the parties involved.

mercantilism A system of trade between colonies and their home nation.

militia A military force drawn from the civilian population.

monarchy Government by a ruler who usually reigns by heredity and for life.

mutiny Rebellion against authority.

nobility A class of high breeding and rank.

parliament A legislature or council where laws are made.

preamble An introductory statement that explains a document's purpose.

privateer A private ship taken over by the government in times of war.

ratify To approve.

reconciliation Reestablishing a close relationship.

repeal To take back.

treaty A formal agreement between two or more nations.

tyranny A government whose leader has absolute power over the people.

FOR MORE INFORMATION

American Independence Museum
One Governor's Lane
Exeter, NH 03833
(603) 772-2622
Web site: http://www.independencemuseum.org

Independence National Historical Park
143 South Third Street
Philadelphia, PA 19106
(215) 597-8974
Web site: http://www.nps.gov/inde

Old Barracks Museum
Barrack Street
Trenton, NJ 08608
(609) 396-1776
Web site: http://www.barracks.org

Web Site
Due to the changing nature of Internet links, the Rosen Publishing
Group, Inc., has developed an online list of Web sites related to the
subject of this book. This site is updated regularly. Please use this
link to access the list:

http://www.rosenlinks.com/psah/coco

# FOR FURTHER READING

Bober, Natalie S. *Countdown to Independence: A Revolution of Ideas in England and Her American Colonies 1760-1776.* New York: Atheneum, 2001.

Meltzer, Milton. *The American Revolutionaries: A History in Their Own Words 1750-1800.* New York: Thomas Y. Crowell, 1987.

Oberle, Lora Polack. *The Declaration of Independence.* Mankato, MN: Bridgestone Books, 2002.

Washburne, Carolyn. *A Multicultural Portrait of Colonial Life.* New York: Marshall Cavendish, 1993.

Young, Alfred F., Terry Fife, and Mary E. Janzen. *We the People: Voices and Images of the New Nation.* Philadelphia: Temple University Press, 1993.

BIBLIOGRAPHY

Allison, Robert J., ed. *American Eras: Revolutionary Era, 1754–1783*. Detroit: Gale, 1998.

Burnett, Edmund C. *The Continental Congress*. New York: MacMillan, 1941.

Burnett, Edmund C., ed. *Letters of Members of the Continental Congress*. Gloucester, MA: P. Smith, 1963.

Greene, Jack, and J. R. Pole, eds. *The Blackwell Encyclopedia of the American Revolution*. Cambridge, MA: Blackwell, 1991.

Sanders, Jennings B. *Evolution of the Departments of the Continental Congress 1774–1789*. Chapel Hill, NC: University of North Carolina Press, 1935.

Smith, Paul H. *Letters of Delegates to Congress, 1774–1789*, Volumes 1–26. Washington, DC: Library of Congress, 1980.

Tourtellot, Arthur B. "... we mutually pledge to each other our Lives, our Fortunes, and our Sacred Honor." *American Heritage* 14 (1), December 1962, pp. 36–41.

PRIMARY SOURCE IMAGE LIST

Page 13: Page from the Stamp Act of 1765. Printed in London by Mark Baskett in 1766. Housed in the Library of Congress.

Page 14: *Boston Tea Party*, by W. D. Cooper. Engraving from 1789. Housed in the Library of Congress.

Page 17: *The First Continental Congress, Carpenters' Hall, Philadelphia, 1774.* Oil on canvas. Painted by Clyde O. DeLand. Housed in the Atwater Kent Museum in Philadelphia.

Page 18: Portrait of George III, king of Great Britain. Engraved by G. S. and G. J. Facius after a portrait by William Berczy. Published in 1791. Housed in the National Library of Australia.

Page 22: The Petition of the First Continental Congress to King George III. October 26, 1774. Handwritten by John Dickinson. Housed in the Library of Congress.

Page 27: Working copy of the Olive Branch Petition, 1775. Preserved in the Karpeles Manuscript Library in Santa Barbara, California. Originals are housed in the New York Public Library and the Public Record Office in London.

Page 29: Engraving of the Continental army from *Harper's Weekly*, 1877. Created after a work by Julian Scott.

Page 35: Draft fragment of the Declaration of Independence. Written by Thomas Jefferson in June 1776. Housed in the Library of Congress.

Page 37: *The First Public Reading of the Declaration of Independence.* Illustration by Eugene Lawrence after a drawing by Howard Pyle. Published in *Harper's Weekly* in 1880. From a private collection.

Page 38: Declaration of Independence. Printed on July 4, 1776, by John Dunlap. Housed in the Library of Congress.

Page 43: George Washington's commission as commander in chief of the Continental army. June 19, 1775. Housed in the Library of Congress.

Page 45: Front and back of a five-dollar Continental. From September 26, 1778. Printed by Hall and Sellers in Philadelphia. Signed by Joseph Walter and Lewis Farmer.

Page 47: Treaty of Paris, 1783. Housed in the National Archives.

Page 50: Articles of Confederation, 1777. Housed in the National Archives.

Page 53: Constitution of United States, 1787. Housed in the National Archives.

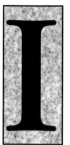

INDEX

About the Author

Betty Burnett is a Connecticut Yankee who grew up hearing stories of the Revolutionary War in New England. She is the author of a dozen books of history and now lives in St. Louis, Missouri.

Photo Credits

Front cover, back cover (top left), p. 31 © Bettman/Corbis; back cover (top right, middle right), pp. 1, 11 © Hulton/Archive/Getty Images; back cover (middle left) Pilgrim Hall Museum; back cover (bottom left), p. 37 © The Bridgeman Art Library; back cover (bottom right) William T. Clements Library, University of Michigan; p. 5 courtesy of The General Libraries, The University of Texas at Austin; pp. 13, 22, 43 Manuscript Division, Library of Congress; p. 14 Rare Book and Special Collections Division, Library of Congress; p. 17 © Atwater Kent Museum of Philadelphia/The Bridgeman Art Library; p. 18 © National Library of Australia, Canberra, Australia/The Bridgeman Art Library; p. 25 Delaware Art Museum, Willmington/The Bridgeman Art Library; p. 27 courtesy Karpeles Manuscript Library Museums; p. 29 Library of Congress/The Bridgeman Art Library; p. 35 Thomas Jefferson Papers, Manuscript Division, Library of Congress; pp. 38, 47, 50, 53, National Archives and Records Administration; p. 45 The Robert H. Gore, Jr. Numismatic Collection, Department of Special Collections, University of Notre Dame Libraries.

Designer: Nelson Sá; Editor: Christine Poolos; Photo Researcher: Adriana Skura